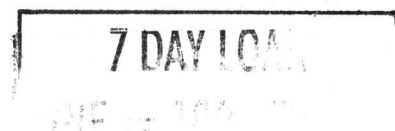
Because I'm Special

A take-home programme to enhance
self-esteem in children aged 6 to 9

Margaret Collins

Lucky Duck is more than a publishing house and training agency. George Robinson and Barbara Maines founded the company in the 1980s when they worked together as a head and psychologist developing innovative strategies to support challenging students.

They have an international reputation for their work on bullying, self-esteem, emotional literacy and many other subjects of interest to the world of education.

George and Barbara have set up a regular news-spot on the website. Twice yearly these items will be printed as a newsletter. If you would like to go on the mailing list to receive this then please contact us:

e-mail newsletter@luckyduck.co.uk   website www.luckyduck.co.uk

ISBN 1 873 942 54 0

Published by Lucky Duck Publishing Ltd.

www.luckyduck.co.uk

Commissioning editor: George Robinson
Edited by Sara Perraton
Designed by Andy Smith
Illustrated by Philippa Drakeford
Printed by Antony Rowe Limited

Reprinted June 2004

© Margaret Collins 2002

Contents

Acknowledgements

Noreen Wetton–a constant inspiration, Colleagues at the Health Education Unit, Research and Graduate School of Education University of Southampton, for support.

George Robinson - who edits so brilliantly.

How to use the CD-ROM

The CD-ROM contains a PDF file labelled 'Worksheets.pdf' which contains worksheets for each session in this resource. You will need Acrobat Reader version 3 or higher to view and print these pages.

The document is set up to print to A4 but you can enlarge the pages to A3 by increasing the output percentage at the point of printing using the page set-up settings for your printer.

Alternatively, you can photocopy the pages directly from this book.

Introduction

Why do we need to promote positive self-esteem?

Here are some quotes from: *Promoting Children's Mental Health within Early Years and School Settings*, DfEE 2001.

"Mental health is about maintaining a good level of personal and social functioning For children and young people, this means getting on with others, both peers and adults, participating in educative and other social activities, and having a **positive self-esteem**.*"*

Page 1 states that children who are mentally healthy have been defined as "having the ability to initiate, develop and sustain mutually satisfying personal relationships' and 'become aware of others and empathise with them".

Pages 3 to 5 highlight the notion that certain children have particular vulnerabilities or risk factors which we need to balance against their 'assets' or their resiliences. Risk factors in the child include 'low self-esteem'. Resilience seems to involve several related elements i.e: a sense of self-esteem and confidence, secondly a belief in one's own self-efficacy and ability to deal with changes and adaptation and thirdly a repertoire of social problem solving approaches'.

Page 26 refers to disruptive children who, having difficulties reading the behaviour of other children, can believe that this is hostile or negative and respond accordingly. Work to help children read the signals of people around them and respond in a more positive manner 'has been shown to have long-term preventative effects for such children'.

Promoting self-esteem is worthwhile. Do we sometimes forget to acknowledge and praise improved human qualities as being as important as academic success? It is difficult to measure and reward children's increasing personal skills.

Motivation–the challenge to succeed is within us. If we are successful we go on to more productive learning. If we fail, what happens? Many give up and try something else. So it is with children. Many young learners who experience constant failure or censure go on to become even more reluctant learners. Children who constantly fail or who feel that they are 'no good' need help to experience success that will raise their self-esteem. Teachers can do a lot towards this in the classroom. But parents, if they are allowed to become actively involved, can do so much more at home.

Children who have positive self-esteem can more easily resist persuasion, peer pressure and bullying. This will become more important as the children grow into adolescence and have to face temptations such as early sexual activity, smoking, alcohol and drug abuse. Those with good self-esteem are more able to talk to people about these teenage issues, accept advice and make up their own mind about how to act.

A child who has good self-esteem is able to stand up and say "NO".

As adults we tend to do the things we are good at and avoid the things we are bad at. In school, we find the things that children can't do e.g. read–and make them do more of it! No sooner have they reached a target than we push them on to the next.

How can we do it?

So how are we going to do all this with large classes and so much to teach? It can be done through circle time and classroom activities which are also teaching several other skills, as in *Because We're Worth it* Collins, M (2001) These issues are addressed through the activities in this book.

It can also be achieved through a planned parent partnership with parents working with their children.

The following paragraph is taken from *Because We're Worth it.* (ibid)–a book of activities for teachers to use in schools, devised to enhance self-esteem among their pupils.

"It is not always easy to help young children to feel good about themselves. All too often they are told that they are not good, they are 'not old enough' they, have done this or that wrong. How must it feel to be a young child at the mercy of all powerful adults? Can you remember your feelings when, as a young child, you had made a mistake or done something wrong, and how daunting it was to face up to the 'giants' who had control over you?"

Following the publication of *Because We're Worth it* it was felt that a set of activity sheets for the children to start work on in school and finish off at home would be a useful extension of work done in school, It would also enable parents/families to have some idea of what their children were doing in school and to recognise the importance of families as promoters of self-esteem in their children at home. It was not intended that the children would return the sheets to school–to be marked–but keep them at home (although teachers are at liberty to decide otherwise!).

From these original thoughts, we realised that other schools not using *Because We're Worth it* would be interested in a book that involved parents and made them more aware of the importance of self-esteem. Schools who are promoting parent partnership would find these activity sheets a good link activity.

There is also a third use. Teachers have said that a good worksheet will make a good lesson. Without using *Because We're Worth it*, teachers can use the ideas from each activity sheet as a class lesson, and then ask children to use the activity sheet in school as a record or extension of the work or send it home for parents to use with their children.

This book of activity sheets therefore provides for three models of use:

- ▶ As a school (or home) extension to work done in school to follow up the activities suggested in *Because We're Worth it*

- ▶ As a set of activity sheets for teachers to send home from time to time for parents to use with their children as part of a 'parent partnership' initiative – i.e. without direct work being first done in school

- ▶ As a home extension to teacher - organised work done in school around the theme of each activity sheet.

The purpose of sending the sheets home is to encourage parents/carers to follow the same route in promoting self-esteem in their children. Many parents/carers are busy and hard-working and have little time to stop and think that what they say and do with their children has a great impact on their children's lives. What they do **not** say and what they do **not** do has just as much impact.

How many times are we all guilty of seeing the difficulties, disorder and untidiness instead of the good that is there? We notice what has not been done instead of what has been done. Poor qualities stand out and good qualities go unnoticed. We thus ignore the good and censure the bad.

If we include parents and families in this work of promoting self-esteem, we will broaden the boundaries of the work. Try it and see.

▶ Model 1: Extension to activities found in Because We're Worth it.

The activity sheets follow the same format as the book in that there are activity sheets to use during or after completing each of the 10 sections of the book in school, with six activity sheets for each section. Naturally because of the over-arching theme of self-esteem, there is considerable overlap.

The sheets can be photocopied and used in any order, according to their relationship with the work done in class, or they can stand alone. You may wish to ignore the first two pages in each section (as they are intended to be sent home to the parent before the activity sheets). Each set of activities has a cartoon face at the top. This will help those of you who are using the book to match the activity sheets to the activities in the book. The earlier sheets in each section are the simplest and have been designed with younger or less able children in mind.

You will need to explain to the children that these activity sheets are to be taken home to finish off and to show to their families and that you do not require the children to return them. You could suggest that you expect them to do their very best work for this very reason. Once families have seen the first 'take home' sheet, you could suggest that children make a home folder to put them in or suggest that they display each one in their personal space at home – replacing each old one with the latest.

You will need to help children who are early readers by reading the whole sheet through with the children before they start to do them. If you want the children to do the sheets after finishing other work, i.e. at different times, it would be a good idea to stop all the children and read one through to give them an idea of its content. Alternatively, you could encourage peer teaching by suggesting that children visit other children in the class who could read the sheet to them.

Each activity sheet has a list of words to help the children. These are not simply intended as a spelling aid and are deliberately not in an order which would allow children to copy words into blank spaces. Neither are children meant to use all the words. It is hoped that the given words will trigger other more personal and descriptive words for the children to use instead. You can add spellings of other words that the child requires, or for children to 'try out' spellings.

Below the main work on the sheet is an instruction for the child to do some work on the other side of the paper. This piece of work acts as differentiation. It is more personal and can be as short or as long as the child wishes.

At the end of the activity sheet is a reminder to the child to read and check the work and then to sign that s/he has done so. This is another aid to self-esteem –just as painters sign their work, it is hoped that the children will feel proud enough to add their name to their work.

▸ Model 2: Parent partnership

If you are using these activity sheets in this way, you will find in the appendix a suggested format for a first letter to send home to parents. Before each set of six activity sheets you will find a page detailing the rationale for the activities on these sheets, and giving suggestions for the parent in helping their child to complete them. The following page in each section is a suggested cover sheet for the child to complete and decorate. This can be used as the front cover when the six page 'book' has been completed. There is an alternative suggestion for displaying the activity sheets.

▸ Model 3: Homework following a class lesson

If you choose this way of using the activity sheets, you may decide to 'pick and choose' the activities you use and send home the uncompleted activity sheet for the parent to help the child to complete at home. You may still wish to send home the helpful suggestions for getting the most out of the sheet which are on the first page before each section.

Who will benefit from this programme?

The activity sheets have been designed for children in the 6-9 year age group, who are becoming more confident writers and ready to work with less supervision. You may find that some of the easier sheets – the first one or two in each section are suitable for able five year olds. Reluctant learners older than 9 years might enjoy some of the activity sheets.

Children with special needs

Teachers of children with special needs or those working in special schools will find all the activity sheets suitable for raising the self-esteem of these, sometimes vulnerable, children. Teachers can adapt the ideas from the sheets and include them in the child's individual learning programme, with the learning support helper working alongside each child to ensure success.

The activity sheets could be used with older SEN children to work from on their own if the work had first been clearly explained. These could be kept in school as part of the child's portfolio of work. Teachers could also send sheets home for parents to share in the promoting of self-esteem in their child.

Why we need Parents to help –
(you may like to send this page home for parents)

We know that it is important for children to have good self-esteem and to feel that what they do is valued. Some children are good at maths, some at writing, some at sports, art or craft. What we have to do is recognise and value the work and skills of each individual child. We know that children learn more easily and work better if they feel good about themselves and if they know that they are all special in some way.

Right from a child's first days in school, we are trying to help young children to understand the importance of valuing themselves and others. We try to help them to understand and deal with their own feelings and emotions. We give opportunities for them to co-operate with other children in work and play. We try to help children to respect other people's emotions and feelings.

We help them to learn, too, that everything they do can have a consequence for themselves as well as for other people. We help them to develop the skills they need to form relationships.

All these skills depend on good self-esteem and good self-esteem depends on them. If we can develop these skills in children, we go a long way towards giving them a firm foundation for their future adult lives, as useful, caring, sensitive and fulfilled citizens.

Raising self-esteem among children will only work if all adults – teachers, parents, carers and others – take care about the self-esteem of other people. Children see much more than we realise and will quickly tune in to a feeling of a lack of respect among adults, or lack of care about each others' feelings.

We will be working with the children on developing their self-esteem through lessons and through some activity sheets that the children will bring home. We hope that you will help your children with the work on these activity sheets, talk around each theme and show your child that you value their work. These activity sheets are yours to keep. You may like your child to keep some of them in a folder or display them in their personal space in their own room.

You may also like to ask parents to come to your classroom to talk about the issues raised about doing the work at home and about the content of the activity sheets.

There are various suggested letters in the appendix. You can involve the children by asking them to decorate the border or add their name.

You can photocopy the letter(s) or use the ideas to create your own school specific note to parents.

What you get in this book

There are 10 sets of take home sheets. The section titles correspond to the words in the speech bubbles on each sheet and will facilitate identification of the sets. (The words in brackets correspond to the speech bubble on the sheets in that section.)

There is obviously considerable overlap and some activity sheets could be used to reinforce work under other headings.

▸ **Self-Identity**

(What's your name?)
Names are important to us
What's your name?
Hey You!
What shall I call you?
Meeting and greeting
Nobody

▸ **Self-Worth**

(I'm worth it)
I feel great
I try hard
I feel sad when…
Feeling good
Things I like
Praise me

▸ **Friendships**

(My friends are fun)
Sam's friend
I value my friends
Family friends
Pet friends
Friendship groups
Good advice

▸ **Body Language**

(Watch me!)
I'm proud of myself
I feel sad
Picture this
Body speak
Hand signals
Without words

▸ **Intercommunication**

(Let's talk!)
Tell me I'm great
Celebrate
Are you listening?
Listen to me
Let's communicate
Words can hurt

▸ **Feelings**

(How do you feel?)
Today
Jan's party
I feel great
When things go wrong
Zac is fed up
My friend is worried

▸ **Being Confident**

(I can do it!)
I can do this well
Sam and Emil
Good games
A new skill
A good rule for Isa
Well done everyone

▸ **Relationships**

(I'm thinking)
Why I like you
People like me when…
People I trust
Zoz needs help
Is this bullying?
Under the surface

▸ **Empathy and Sympathy**

(I can feel it)
Someone new
Missing him
We can help
How do they feel?
Poor Jo
In someone else's place

▸ **Co-operation**

(We work together)
This is my group
We help each other
I work with my family
Keep to the rules
Rules of friendship
Celebrate success

At the end of the book there is a list of picture storybooks that you may like
to use with the children. You will have most of these books in school, but when
re-reading them you can focus on the self-esteem element.

Self-Identity

This section contains: parents' notes,
a cover sheet for children to decorate,
and the following activities:

- ▶ Names are important to us
- ▶ What's your name?
- ▶ Hey You!
- ▶ What shall I call you?
- ▶ Meeting and greeting
- ▶ Nobody

Self-Identity

Parents' Notes

These activities aim to help children to recognise the importance of remembering and using people's names. To remember people's names is a confidence booster in itself. Children need to know how to greet people and that it is polite to use people's names when speaking to them.

This section contains the following activities:

- Names are important to us
- What's your name?
- Hey You!
- What shall I call you?
- Meeting and greeting
- Nobody

First encourage your child to decorate and colour the enclosed cover sheet. We suggest that as you receive each activity sheet you find time to sit down in a quiet place with your child and read it through together. Help your child to understand and remember the words in the word list and use this list to write in spellings of other words your child chooses to use. You will find that some sections suggest ways to enhance the work on the sheet with ideas for you to talk about with your child.

▸ **Names are important**
Talk with your child about why it is polite to use people's names, and how we feel when people use our names. Tell your child why you chose their name.

▸ **What's your name**
Explain to your child the need for titles – that it is polite to call people 'Mr. So and so' until you know them well enough to call them by their first name. Talk to them about the ways we address people in other countries.

▸ **Hey You!**
Talk to your child about how people could feel if we misuse their name or if we call them unkind names. Some children are very happy when people give them a nickname but others can find it hateful. Talk about this to your child and explain that we are all entitled to be called by a name we like.

▸ **What shall I call you?**
Explain to your child that there are important people who have very special titles and that there are laid down ways to use these titles. We need to know the right way to use these titles if we are to feel confident about talking to them.

- **Meeting and greeting**

  Encourage your child to feel confident about greeting people. Saying "Good morning Mum/Dad/Mrs Jones" is a good start to the day. Children who are able to look people in the eye and greet them in an appropriate way show that they have good self-esteem.

- **Nobody**

  Nothing diminishes a child's self-esteem more than being told that they are unimportant, silly or stupid. Make sure that your child knows s/he is important in your family. This activity was sparked off by the book *Nothing* by Mike Inkpen. S/he will probably know the book from school, but you might like to borrow it from the library to read again to your child.

Self-Identity

This is me. My name is ....

Names are important to us
What's your name?
Hey You!
What shall I call you?
Meeting and greeting
Nobody

Names are important to us

Draw a picture of yourself and write your name.

My name is...

How long have you had your name?

I have had my name for .... years

Who gave you your name?

....gave me my name.

When is your birthday?

My birthday is..

How do you feel when people use your name?

I feel ....

Draw a picture of your family.

Words to help me:
mummy
family
great
big
happy
proud
daddy
carer

I have read and checked my work carefully.

Signed...date..........................

What's your name?

The first words babies learn to speak are usually names of the people in their family. Write down the first names of some people who live in your house.

....

We know it is important to address people correctly.

In Britain, for men we use the title Mister and write it Mr.

For married women we use.....................................

For girls we say ....

For boys we say...

In France, Mr Green would be Monsieur Green.

His wife would be called ....

His daughter would be ....

In Spain, Mr Brown would be Senor Brown.

His wife would be ....

His daughter would be ....

Words to help me:
Mr
Mrs
Ms
Master
Miss
Senora
Senorita
Madame
Mademoiselle

Turn over the page and draw a picture of a yourself. Write your full name and title. How do you feel when people use your full name and title?

I have read and checked my work carefully.

Signed...date..........................

Hey You!

Sometimes we meet people and we don't know their names. What is the best thing to do? Tick the one you think best from this list. Put a cross against the worst. You could:

☐ Just not use a name when you speak to them.

☐ Say, "Hey you."   ☐ Say, "I'm…Who are you?"

☐ Ignore them altogether   ☐ Say, "What are you called?"

☐ Say, "I think I know you, but I don't know your name."

☐ Ask a friend what the person is called.

What would you say if you always called someone Steven and you heard someone call him Steve? I would say ……………………………………………………………………………………

What would you say if you heard someone call a girl an unkind name, e.g. "Shorty"? I would say ……………………………………………………………………………………

Do you like your own name?   yes ☐   no ☐

If you had to have another first name added to yours, what name would you choose? Why?

I would choose ………………………………………because………………………

Turn over the page and draw a picture of two friends.

Write their names underneath.

Do they ever use nicknames for you and each other?

How do you feel if they use these nicknames?

I have read and checked my work carefully.

Signed…………………………………………………date…………………………

Words to help me:
like
feel
nickname
think
feelings
careful

What shall I call you?

It can make you feel good to know the correct way to address certain people. Try to finish these sentences.

When speaking to your teacher you say...

When speaking to the headteacher you say...

When speaking to a neighbour you say...

When speaking to a doctor you say ....

How do you like people to speak to you? ....

Using people's names correctly is important for you and them.

How do you feel when people misuse your name?

....

What do you say? ....

Can you find out what people say when they meet important people such as a police officer, someone at church, royalty or a prime minister? What do they say when meeting these people?

Write here what you find out.

....

....

Words to help me:
Miss
Mrs
Mr
Sir
Father
Vicar
Majesty
Doctor - Dr.

Turn over the page and draw a picture of yourself meeting an important person. What are you saying to them? Use a speech bubble to write what you are saying.

I read and checked my work carefully.

Signed...date...........................

Meeting and greeting

There are many ways to greet people when you meet them for the first time.

Write down as many as you can remember...

....

How do you greet people
in your family each morning?

Make a chart in these boxes.

Person	What I say
....	....
....	....
....	....
....	....

Words to help me:
mummy,
family,
great,
big,
happy,
proud,
daddy

Draw yourself meeting your best friend in the school playground.

How do you greet each other?

Turn over and draw yourself
meeting and greeting someone
new.

Who are you meeting? Write
down how you feel. about it.

I have read and checked my work carefully.

Signed...date ....

Nobody

Read this story:

Some children were playing together and a little girl was all alone, watching them.

One boy said, "Who's that?" and a big girl said,

"Oh that's nobody – come on let's get on with our game."

And they did.

Draw 'Nobody'

How do you think 'Nobody' felt?

....

What do you think 'Nobody' could say or do?

....

Can you think of a good ending for this story?

A good ending would be...

....

....

....

Turn over the page and draw a picture of a person who is the opposite of Nobody, someone special, unique or famous. Call the person 'Somebody'.

Words to help me:
sad
unhappy worthless
useless lonely
great
smiling
wanted
opposite
unique

Write a story about yourself feeling great – like 'Somebody'. Write what you did that made you feel like that and what people said about you.

I read and checked my work carefully.

Signed..date.........................

Self-Worth

This section contains: parents' notes, a cover sheet for children to decorate and the following activities.

- ▸ I feel great
- ▸ I try hard
- ▸ I feel sad when…
- ▸ Feeling good
- ▸ Things I like
- ▸ Praise me

Self-Worth

Parents' Notes

These activities aim to help children to value themselves. They focus very positively on the things they are good at doing and ways to make themselves feel better when they are not feeling good.

First encourage your child to decorate and colour the enclosed cover sheet. We suggest that as you receive each activity sheet, you find time to sit down in a quiet place with your child and read through it together. Help your child to understand and remember the words in the word list and use this list to write in spellings of other words your child chooses to use. You will find that some sections suggest ways to enhance the work on the sheet with ideas for you to talk about with your child.

This section contains the following activities:

- I feel great
- I try hard
- I feel sad when…
- Feeling good
- Things I like
- Praise me

▸ **I feel great**

This is a simple sheet and your child won't need much help, but try to find time to discuss the things that make your child feel great, how s/he feels when people say positive things and the kind of encouraging things s/he likes to hear. Do you have a special word in your family that you use when you are pleased with your child – such as 'brill' or 'splendido'

▸ **I try hard**

It helps children if they feel they can talk about good and bad times with a parent. Can you try to find a time in each day when it is OK for your child to come and talk about such things? Perhaps just before going to sleep is a good time to talk through the day and allow your child to open up about good (and bad) things that have happened.

▸ **I feel sad when…**

Talk about the kinds of things that will cheer your child up when s/he feels low. Can you suggest some? Talk about what you and other people in your family do when you feel low. Encourage your child to understand that everyone feels low at times. A good thing to do is to look in a mirror and make a face at yourself – it's almost bound to make you smile!

- ▶ **Feeling good**

  Talking through this activity sheet will help you to realise how important it is for your child to hear you say 'well done' – even if it is for a very small thing they have done well!

- ▶ **Things I like**

  Help your child to focus on the things s/he and you like there are lots of things to talk about around this activity sheet

- ▶ **Praise me**

  It is so easy to be negative – we need to catch the good and praise it. You may need to suggest some things your child has done well at home today, e.g. got up when called, dressed self, ate up, cleared up, tidied up, helped! Talk about all these ways of giving praise and relate them to what you say and do in your family. Talk about how you yourself like to be praised as well.

Self-Worth

This is me feeling that I am special.

I feel great
I try hard
I feel sad when…
Feeling good
Things I like
Praise me

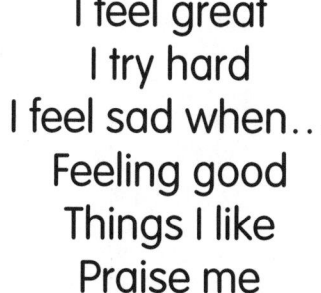

I feel great

Draw a picture of you when you feel great.

This is me. I feel great.

I feel great when ....

....

....

I feel great when people say ....

....

Draw your best toy. Write about it.

....

....

....

I have read my work and checked it carefully.

Signed...date........................

Words to help me:
happy
well
good
super
things
right
wonderful
play
friends

I try hard

Draw a picture of you trying to do your best work.

This is me doing my best work.

When I do my best work I feel

....

....

When it goes wrong I feel

....

....

....

Words to help me:
happy
well
good
wonderful
super
things
unhappy
worried   right
start   again

Turn over the page and design a certificate for people who do good work.

Write your name on it and write what you have done to deserve it

I have read my work and checked it carefully.

Signed..date.........................

I feel sad when...

What makes you feel sad?

I feel sad when someone ....

....

....

What can you do to feel better?

I can ....

What can people say to cheer you up?

They can ....

Draw yourself feeling sad.

Draw someone cheering you up.

Words to help me:
cross
hurt
feelings
play
listen
music
watch

How do you feel now? ....

....

I have read my work and checked it carefully.

Signed...date ....

Feeling good

What can you do that makes you feel good?

I can ....

What do people say to you that makes you feel good?

....

People say ....

....

How do you make your friends feel good?

I ....

What games do you play with your friends
that make you all feel good?

We play ....

What do you do that makes your family feel good
about you?

....

....

Turn over the page and draw yourself with your
family, doing something that will make them say,
'Well done you'.
Write down what you are doing.

I have read my work and checked it carefully.

Signed...date........................

Words to help me:
make   read
play   praise
well done
good work
excellent
sensible
together

Things I like

What I like doing best of all is.................................

....

The people I like to play with best of all are ....

....

The foods I like to eat most are ....

....

The drinks I like best are ....

....

Words to help me:

playing
games
toys
friends

The TV programme I like best is ....

....

Do you feel good when you choose these things?

yes ☐   no ☐

Do you feel good when you let other people choose?

yes ☐   no ☐

Draw yourself choosing
to do something.

Write about your picture here.

....

....

Turn over and draw yourself letting a friend choose
to play a game.

Write about your friend and what you are doing.

Do you feel good? Does your friend feel good?

I read and checked my work carefully.

Signed................   date................

Praise me

Here are two things I have done well at home today.

1. ....

2. ....

Here are two things I did well at school this week.

1. ....

2. ....

When I do things well, I like grown-ups to… (tick the praise you like most)

☐ smile at me

☐ show that you notice it

☐ say, "Well done"

☐ say something else such as ....
....

☐ put a mark on my work

☐ give me a star or ....
....

☐ tell other people

☐ let me do something I really want to do

Turn over and draw yourself being praised for something you did at home.

What did you do? Who praised you?
What was the praise?

I read and checked my work carefully.

Signed................. date.................

Words to help me:

tried hard
thought
careful
tidy
help

Friendships

This section contains: parents' notes, a cover sheet for children to decorate and the following activities.

- ▶ Sam's friend
- ▶ I value my friends
- ▶ Family friends
- ▶ Pet friends
- ▶ Friendship groups
- ▶ Good advice

Friendships

Parents' Notes

These activities aim to help children to recognise the importance of having friends and of being a good friend. Children need to learn that friendship has to be worked at and that it doesn't just happen. There is a lot of sharing and turn taking involved in being a good friend and sometimes children find it is not easy to do either of these.

This section contains the following activities:

- Sam's friend
- I value my friends
- Family friends
- Pet friends
- Friendship groups
- Good advice

First, encourage your child to decorate and colour the enclosed cover sheet. We suggest that as you receive each activity sheet you find time to sit down in a quiet place with your child and read through it together. Help your child to understand and remember the words in the word list and use this list to write in spellings of other words your child chooses to use. You will find that some sections suggest ways to enhance the work on the sheet with ideas for you to talk about with your child.

▸ **Sam's friend**

Here we introduce Sam – who can be girl or boy. It is often easier for a child to stand outside a situation in order to think about it. Talk about the things that good friends do and don't do, and how you know whether a friend is really a good friend.

▸ **I value my friends**

Talk about how important it is to value friends and not to take them for granted. Friendship needs to be worked at and young children may need help to realise this. Talk about friends of yours that you value and how you do this.

▸ **Family friends**

Your child may not think of members of your family as friends. Encourage your child to think of cousins, aunts and older members of the extended family as friends. Talk about this different kind of friendship and how it can exist even though they may meet only rarely. Borrow *Orlando's little while friends* (A Wood) from the library and read it with your child.

- **Pet friends**

  Talk about pets as friends – pets need love and care just as human friends do. Talk about people you know who have pets as friends – and those who have dogs who help them in their lives. Talk about your own pet ,if you have one, and its needs.

- **Friendship groups**

  Here's Sam again, who belongs to many groups. Talk about friendship groups to your child and ask her/him to write down in the list all the groups s/he belongs to. Then, using three of their own groups, help your child to write the names of the friends who belong to these groups. (If your child doesn't belong to any groups, just use school, class and family.)

- **Good advice**

  This activity puts your child in control – giving advice to Sam. You can talk here about all the options for mending friendships. In essence, someone has to say 'sorry' and each has to meet the other halfway.

Friendships

This is me being a good friend.

Sam's friend
I value my friends
Family friends
Pet friends
Friendship groups
Good advice

Sam's friend

Sam says, "My friends are fun."

Draw a picture of Sam's friend.

Words to help me:
playing
running
sharing
being
kind
thinking

What is Sam's friend doing?

Sam's friend is..

....

How do you know that this is a good friend?

A good friend...

....

Turn over and draw yourself and some friends playing together.

What are you playing? How do you feel?

I read and checked my work carefully.

Signed...date...........

I value my friends

I help my friends when I...

....

I share with my friends when.................................

....

I show I like my friend when I ....

....

Words to help me:
choose
first
plays
thinks
kind
helpful
shares

Draw a friend here.

What do they do to show they are
a friend?

....

....

....

Turn over and draw yourself putting a friend first.

What are you doing? How do you feel?
How does your friend feel?

I read and checked my work carefully

Signed..date ....

Family friends

Words to help me:
brother
sister
cousin
aunt
baby
Grandma
Grandad

Draw your family friends here.

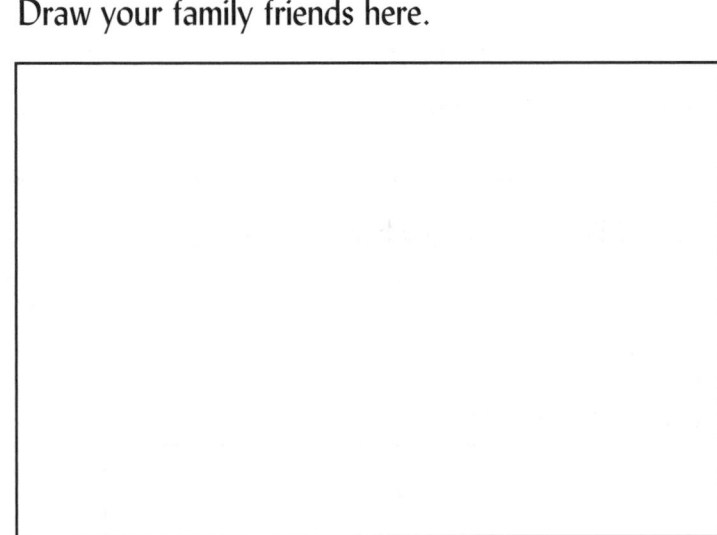

My family friends are called

....

My family friends are fun because

....

Some family friends live far away. Who are they?
They are...

....

Turn over and draw yourself playing with family friends who live far away.

Where are you? When do you see these friends?

I read and checked my work carefully.

Signed...date...........................

Pet friends

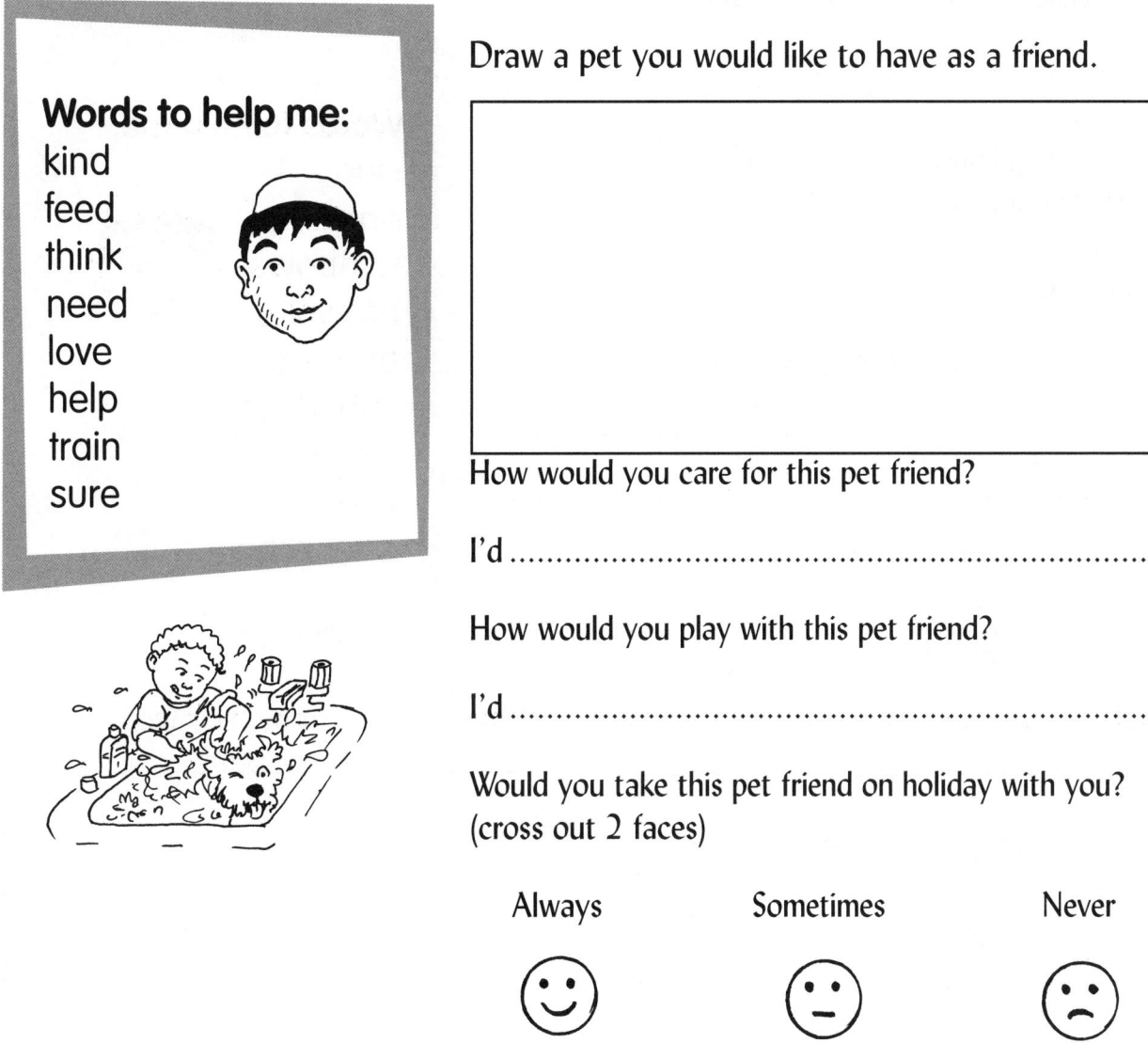

Words to help me:
kind
feed
think
need
love
help
train
sure

Draw a pet you would like to have as a friend.

How would you care for this pet friend?

I'd ....

How would you play with this pet friend?

I'd ....

Would you take this pet friend on holiday with you?
(cross out 2 faces)

Always	Sometimes	Never
☺	😐	☹

How would you care for it then?

I'd ....

Turn over and draw a pet friend you know.

Who takes care of this pet? How do they show they love it?

I read and checked my work carefully.

Signed..date........................

Friendship groups

Some children belong to these friendship groups.

- class
- family
- swimming church
- neighbourhood
- football
- gym club

Write your own friendship groups here.

1 ....

2 ....

3 ....

4 ....

Words to help me:
club
dancing
rainbows
brownies
beavers
cub scouts
music
choir
after school club

Make a list of some friends in two of your friendship groups – draw their faces.

These friends are in my

.................................group

These friends are in my

.................................group

Are some of your friends in more than one friendship group? yes ☐   no ☐

Turn over the page and draw yourself in one of your friendship groups having fun with these friends.

What are you doing? How do you feel? How do your friends feel?

I read and checked my work carefully.

Signed...date........................

Good advice

Read this story:

Sam quarrelled with a good friend. They both wanted to be friends again, but didn't know how to do it.

What advice would you give to Sam?

I would say ....

....

Sam took your advice and wants to know how to prevent quarrels in future.

I would say ....

....

Words to help me:
sorry
didn't mean it
won't do it again
think ahead
stop
remember
words
hurt
feelings

Turn over and draw Sam making up with the friend.

What is Sam saying? What is the friend saying? How do they both feel now?

I read and checked my work carefully.

Signed...date.........................

Body Language

This section contains: parents' notes, a cover sheet for children to decorate and the following activities.

- ▶ I'm proud of myself
- ▶ I feel sad
- ▶ Picture this
- ▶ Body speak
- ▶ Hand signals
- ▶ Without words

Body Language

Parents' Notes

These activities aim to help children to recognise that people's bodies are always telling the world about their feelings. It is sometimes hard for children to understand what body language is telling them. It is often easy for them to misunderstand other people's feelings unless they put them into words. These activities can help children to understand the importance of talking about their feelings and not relying on their body language to tell the full story. At the same time, they can become more aware of what their body is telling other people. Ask them to practise looking proud, in control, confident – to practise stretching tall and looking people in the eye.

First encourage your child to decorate and colour the enclosed cover sheet. We suggest that as you receive each activity sheet, you find time to sit down in a quiet place with your child and read through it together. Help your child to understand and remember the words in the word list and use this list to write in spellings of other words your child chooses to use. You will find that some sections suggest ways to enhance the work on the sheet with ideas for you to talk about with your child.

This section contains the following activities:

- I'm proud of myself
- I feel sad
- Picture this
- Body speak
- Hand signals
- Without words

▶ **I'm proud of myself**
  This kind of pride is not one of the seven deadly sins! Pride in their work, appearance and ability to cope is to be encouraged. Remind your child of occasions when s/he has made you proud – s/he may need help in thinking of these times. Talk about what happened and how it made <u>you</u> feel. Ask them how they look to other people when they feel proud of something they have done.

▶ **I feel sad**
  Talk about the posture of people who are sad – round shoulders, eyes down, loose limbs. Play about with these body attitudes before the child starts the sheet. Talk about the things that cheer you up and make you feel better.

▶ Picture this

It is not easy to draw pictures of people's body language, but it is a good thing to try! Make a game of acting out how you look when you are excited, scared, worried or glad before starting the activity sheet. You may need to help by showing how to change the features or faces of people – mouth turned down, eyebrows tilting, frown lines.

▶ Body speak

This activity asks the children to think of how they use their face and body to 'talk' to people without words. They use this kind of language at school and in play. They 'give five', shrug shoulders, wave, pull faces, mime attitudes. You might like to play around with all these gestures before starting the activity sheet.

▶ Hand signals

This activity sheet extends the previous one, this time asking your child to think only of hand signals – pointing a finger, shaking a fist, thumbs up and down. Again, play around with these and other hand gestures before doing the drawing and writing.

▶ Without words

This final activity sheet brings together much of what your child has been learning about the importance of interpreting body language correctly. Act out some of these postures and try to guess what your child is trying to convey. Remind your child that someone who feels good about her/himself will walk tall, look people in the eye and smile to convey their confidence.

Body Language

This is how my body looks when
I am feeling great

I'm proud of myself
I feel sad
Picture this
Body speak
Hand signals
Without words

I'm proud of myself

Think of something you have done that made you feel proud of yourself.

What did you do? ....

Why did you do it?

I did it because...

....

Draw yourself feeling proud of yourself.

Words to help me:
helped
thought
worked
cared
tried
practised

How did other people feel?

....

Turn over and draw someone being proud of you. How can we tell they are proud of you?

I read and checked my work carefully.

Signed...date ....

When I feel sad

This is me feeling sad.

Words to help me:
long
tearful
unsmiling
hard
closed
hunched
quiet
soft

You can tell I feel sad because my face ....

....

Because my body is...

....

Because my voice is ....

....

How will we know when you feel better?

....

....

....

Turn over and draw pictures of what you do to make yourself feel
better when you are sad.

I read and checked my work carefully.

Signed..date.......................

Picture this

Can you draw pictures of people who feel like this?

This person is very excited because they are going on holiday.	This person is very scared because they heard a noise in the night.
This person is very worried because they have forgotten to take something to school.	This person is glad because they are going to a party today.

How do people show how they feel?

Excited people ....

Scared people ....

Worried ....

Glad ....

Turn over and write a letter to someone who is very excited about coming to visit you.Draw a picture of how you look you when you meet.

I read and checked my work carefully.

Signed...date.........................

Body speak

We use parts of our body to speak to people.

We nod and shake our head, raise our eyebrows.

Draw pictures of 4 body speaks you use to 'talk' to your friends (e.g. wave your hand, shake your head, slap hands, raise eyebrows, beckon). Write what they are.

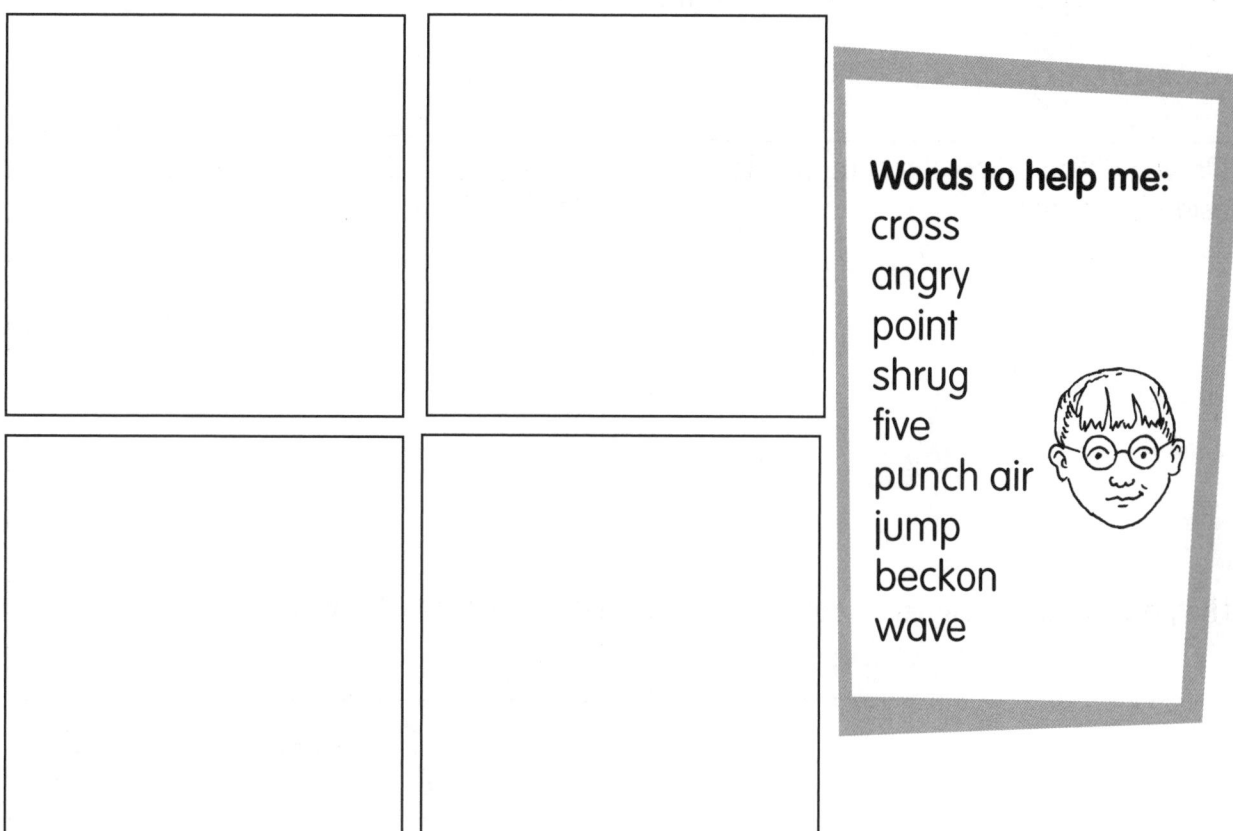

Words to help me:
cross
angry
point
shrug
five
punch air
jump
beckon
wave

Turn over and draw yourself giving a 'come to me' sign to a friend.

How do you feel when your friend understands you?

I read and checked my work carefully.

Signed..date ....

Hand signals

Think about people who signal using their hands.

What do people mean when they put their thumb up?

They mean..

What do people mean when they put their thumb down?

They mean..

What do people mean when they put both their fists up in the air?

They mean..

Draw a police officer directing traffic using hand signals.	Draw a football referee at a match using hand signals.
The police officer's signals mean	The ref's signals mean.......................... ....

Turn over and draw some friends making friendly hand signals.

How do you feel when you know what they mean?

I read and checked my work carefully.

Signed..
date..

Words to help me:
turning
right
left
slowing
come on
don't move
that's wrong
penalty

Without words – how can you tell?

How can you tell when a person in your family is cross?

I can tell when ....is cross

because ....

How can you tell when a friend is sad?

I can tell when..is sad

because ....

How can you tell when a toddler you know is excited?

I can tell when...is excited

because ....

How can you tell when a grown-up you know is worried?

I can tell when ....is worried

because ....

Words to help me:
face
eyes
frown
mouth
down
jumping
clap hands
hug
cuddle
kiss

Turn over and write a letter to a person in your family about the body language they use when they are pleased with you. How does that make you feel?

I read and checked my work carefully.

Signed...date ....

Intercommunication

This section contains: parents' notes,
a cover sheet for children to decorate
and the following activities.

- ▸ Tell me I'm great
- ▸ Celebrate
- ▸ Are you listening
- ▸ Listen to me
- ▸ Let's communicate
- ▸ Words can hurt

Intercommunication

Parent's Notes

These activities aim to help children to recognise the importance of communication – speaking and listening. The children are asked about the words they like people to use to praise them – language they can use to tell others something good. They are asked to think about how people know that they are really listening and concentrating. They think about communication through touch and how words can hurt.

This section contains the following activities:

- Tell me I'm great
- Celebrate
- Are you listening
- Listen to me
- Let's communicate
- Words can hurt

First, encourage your child to decorate and colour the enclosed cover sheet. We suggest that as you receive each activity sheet, you find time to sit down in a quiet place with your child and read through it together. Help your child to understand and remember the words in the word list and use this list to write in spellings of other words your child chooses to use. You will find that some sections suggest ways to enhance the work on the sheet with ideas for you to talk about with your child.

▶ **Tell me I'm great**
  This activity sheet asks your child to think of how Sam is feeling, helping your child to recognise other people's feelings – the teachers as well as Sam's. It also allows your child to stand outside the situation and think of what pleases teachers and what teachers do and say to encourage children. Talk about this before you start drawing. (You might also talk about what can upset a teacher and how to avoid this!)

▶ **Celebrate**
  This activity helps you and your child to think of the ways people show approval when your child has done something really helpful. Talk about this and about things that have happened when all the family has been full of praise. It helps children to feel good about themselves when they re-live occasions when they have done something really well.

- **Are you listening?**

  Communication is to do with careful listening and here the child is asked to think of ways that people can tell when s/he is listening and concentrating. Children who listen carefully to instructions can usually carry out the tasks they are asked to do correctly -and that helps to build self-esteem.

- **Listen to me?**

  Here, Sam is joined by Jo – Jo can be either a boy or girl. We are asking your child to consider the problem of someone who cannot hear and to think of the implications of this. Someone who cannot hear feels very uncomfortable – both about the lack of hearing and the way other people react. Talk about both these issues with your child and how Sam feels when s/he sticks by Jo.

- **Let's communicate**

  You'll need a dictionary for this one – either a child or adult one will do. Talk about the dictionary explanation so that your child can really understand what it means. This sheet is trying to help children to see that there are other ways of communicating as well as speaking, listening, reading and writing. Talk about how smells and tastes remind you of things that happened. Talk about the value of a hug or a pat to reassure. Ask them how they use their senses to communicate with their friends.

- **Words can hurt**

  Talk about this activity and go through the list of things that a child could do if they see something like this. It is important to use words carefully and make sure that you don't hurt people by thoughtless use of words. Name-calling is bullying. Make sure that your child knows what to do if they witness this. If s/he ignores it, she/he is saying it's OK. If they do something about it, they should feel proud that they have acted correctly.

Intercommunication

This is me talking on the telephone.
I have to listen carefully.

Tell me I'm great
Celebrate
Are you listening
Listen to me
Let's communicate
Words can hurt

Tell me I'm great!

Think about this:

Sam's teacher is very pleased because Sam has done some really good work.

How do you think Sam is feeling?

I think Sam is feeling...

....

Draw Sam and the teacher here.

Words to help me:
happy
warm
satisfied
glowing
rewarded
well done
tried hard

What is Sam's teacher saying to Sam?

The teacher is saying...

....

Turn over and draw your teacher being pleased with your work.

How do you feel when you have done good work?
What do you say to your family? What do you say to yourself?

I read and checked my work carefully.

Signed...date ....

Celebrate

You have been really helpful at home and your family is pleased.

What do they say to you?

Mum says...

Big sister says ....

Grandma says ....

A friend says...

Words to help me:
well done,
great
thank you
splendid
clever
smart

How does that make you feel?

This makes me feel...

....

You want to celebrate. How will you do this?

I think I will ....

....

Turn over and write a letter to tell a friend about something good that you have done.

Tell them what people said to you. Draw them a picture of what you did.

I read and checked my work carefully.

Signed...date.........................

Are you listening?

Think of the last time your teacher told you a story.

Draw a picture of someone listening to the story.

Words to help me:
still
carefully
looking
thinking
moving
concentrating
eyes
face

How could you tell they were listening?

You could tell they were listening because ....

....

Draw someone who was not listening to the story. What are they doing?

They are ....

Turn over and draw your teacher telling you something. What is your teacher saying to you? How do you feel when you listen well and can remember what was said?

I read and checked my work carefully.

Signed...date ....

Listen to me

Read this story about Sam and Jo and answer the questions.

Sam has a friend called Jo who can't hear very well and has to wear a hearing aid. Sometimes the hearing aid goes wrong.

How can Sam make sure Jo can hear when Sam is talking?

I think Sam can ....

What can Jo do? ....

I think Jo can..

What can Sam do if Jo can't hear the teacher?

I think Sam can ....

It is hard in the playground when Jo can't hear. What can Sam do then?

Some people are unkind to Jo because of the hearing aid. What can Sam do then?

I think Sam can ....

Words to help me:
look
face
clearly
slowly
watch
expression
eyes
write
signal

Turn over and draw Sam and Jo playing in the playground.

What are they playing? How does Jo feel when people say unkind things about people who are deaf? How would you feel if you were Jo? How does Sam feel when he sticks by Jo?

I read and checked my work carefully.

Signed..date........................

Let's communicate

'Communication' is a good word. What does it mean? Use a dictionary and write down the meaning here.

Communicate means ....

....

You can communicate to yourself and others through your five senses, when you *hear, see, smell, taste, touch.*

Finish these sentences.

When I see my best friend and wave, it means ....

....

When I smell dinner cooking, it means ....

....

When I hear someone crying, I know ....

....

When I taste cakes and nod at Mum, it means ....

....

Words to help me:
hello
dinner
eat
hurt
sad
like
love
happy

When I touch a tiny puppy, it makes me feel ....

....

Turn over and draw someone communicating with you through touch, by giving you a hug.

Who is hugging you? What are they communicating? How do you feel when this person hugs you?

I read and checked my work carefully.

Signed...date........................

Words can hurt

You are in the playground and see a new boy crying because some children said unkind words about him.

You could:

- pretend you didn't see what happened
- carry on playing with your friends
- tell the teacher
- comfort the boy
- ask the new boy to join in your game
- talk to the unkind children who are bigger than you.

Words to help me:
thoughtless
playing
teasing
mean
sorry
think
yourself
name calling
hitting

What do you think is the best thing for you to do? Why?

I will...

....

because ....

....

Someone goes to tell the teacher who calls you all together to talk to you. What do you think the teacher will say?

I think the teacher will say ....

....

The boys say they were only teasing. What will the teacher will say to that?

I think the teacher will say ....

....

Turn over and write what you would say to people who are unkind in the playground. What advice would you give them? How do you feel when you help someone who is unhappy?

I read and checked my work carefully.

Signed...date........................

Feelings

This section contains: parents' notes,
a cover sheet for children to
decorate and the following activities.

- ▶ Today
- ▶ Jan's party
- ▶ I feel great
- ▶ When things go wrong
- ▶ Zac is fed up
- ▶ My friend is worried

Feelings

Parents' notes

These activities aim to help children to increase their vocabulary of feelings so that they have the words to express themselves about their feelings and others. Children who have the language skills to express themselves have more self-confidence.

First, encourage your child to decorate and colour the enclosed cover sheet. We suggest that as you receive each activity sheet, you find time to sit down in a quiet place with your child and read through it together. Help your child to understand and remember the words in the word list and use this list to write in spellings of other words your child chooses to use. You will find that some sections suggest ways to enhance the work on the sheet with ideas for you to talk about with your child.

This section contains the following activities:

- Today
- Jan's party
- I feel great
- When things go wrong
- Zac is fed up
- My friend is worried

▸ **Today**

Talk about feelings and that it is important to be able to talk to someone about them. This first sheet asks the children to identify their feelings today. You may need to help by suggesting more feelings words. When your child has finished the drawing and writing, talk about what has been drawn and written.

▸ **Jan's party**

Here's Jan – a boy or girl – having a party. Your child is asked to think of the feelings of the person having the party, of themselves going to the party, and of Sam who can't go to the party. Talk about how all these children will feel – you may need to help by suggesting feelings words.

▸ **I feel great**

The oval shape is for your child to draw her/himself before writing in the speech bubble how they feel. You may need to add to the suggested words. The 'turn over' activity can be drawn with speech bubbles around the words the people say. (It's hard to get the speech bubble the right size – explain that it is better to write the words before drawing the speech bubble around them.)

‣ When things go wrong

After reading this activity sheet with your child, it would be a good idea to talk about what your child can do to feel better and how you can help when things go wrong. Playing a game, physical or mental, listening to music, a bit of TV, a good book, giving yourself a treat, can all help. Better still is sharing it with a friend you can trust.

‣ Zac is fed up

Meet Zac who is fed up with his family – it's easier for you and your child to talk through Zac's problems and look for solutions than to raise issues within your own family. After talking about Zac's problems, the door is open for you and your child to think about your own situations in a non-threatening way.

‣ My friend is worried

This friend is finding it hard to adjust to temporary change. It's easier to talk over a friend's problem than look for problems in your own family life. Again the door is open to talk about changes that do and must occur as your child grows and as your family situation may change. The 'turn over' activity puts your child in the picture as s/he is in a position to help the friend, and this will make your child feel good about him/herself.

Feelings

This is a picture of me feeling happy and in control of myself.

Today
Jan's birthday
Sam feels great
When things go wrong
Zac is fed up
Sofie is worried

Today

How do you feel today? Why?

Today I feel ....

because ....

This is a picture of how I look today.

Words to help me:
happy
sad
great
worried
anxious
fine

Turn over and draw yourself feeling the opposite.

What makes you feel like this? What do you do when you feel like this?

I read and checked my work carefully.

Signed...date ....

Jan's party

Today it is Jan's birthday and there is
to be a fancy dress party. How does Jan feel?

I think Jan feels ....

because ....

You are going to the party. How do you feel?

I feel ....

Draw yourself dressed up ready for the party

Words to help me:
pleased
excited
nervous
happy
enjoyed
lovely
sad
fed up

I am dressed as a ....

Sam is ill and can't go to the party. How does Sam feel?

I think Sam feels ....

Turn over and draw a card you have made to thank Jan for the party.

How will Jan feel when he gets the card? How do you feel?

I read and checked my work carefully.

Signed...date.........................

I feel great

You have done some really good work today and your teacher is very pleased.

Draw yourself saying how you are feeling

Words to help me:
happy
pleased
walking on air
over the moon
on top of the world
satisfied

I feel ....

....

What will you tell your family about this good work?

I will say ....

....

Draw yourself telling your family about the good work. What will they say to you?

I read and checked my work carefully.

Signed ....date ....

When things go wrong

Think of something that went all wrong for you.

Draw a picture of yourself and write what happened.

Words to help me:
fed up
worried
anxious
scared
cross
angry

This is me when ....

....

How did you feel then? ....

....

What did you do to make yourself feel better? ....

....

What could your family do to help you feel better? ......

....

What could friends do to help you feel better? ....

....

I read and checked my work carefully.

Signed .... date ....

Zac is fed up

Words to help me:
sorry
try harder
forget
careful
think
concentrate
responsible

Draw yourself here giving some advice to Zac.

Hey Zac…

Zac can't get on with his work because he is fed up with his family. He keeps leaving things around and forgetting things and then he gets told off. His work is not good so his teacher is not very pleased.

Zac's friends have some ideas.
They say he could:

- say he's sorry to his family and do nothing

- try harder to remember things

- forget about it and stop worrying

- write a list of things to do, do them and cross them off

- say it doesn't matter anyway

- get things ready before he goes to bed

- organise his things better and keep them tidy

- get on with his work and sort out his problems when he gets home

Turn over and draw Zac at home with his family trying to put things right.

What will Zac say? What will his family say?
How will Zac feel when things are OK again?

I read and checked my work carefully.

Signed..date ....

My friend is worried

Your friend comes to school one day looking worried and you want to help.

What can you do?

I'd ....

What can you say?

I'd say...

Your friend is worried because their Dad has gone to hospital and everything at home is different.

What advice would you give your friend now?

I'd say...

Help your friend to write a 'Get Well' letter to their Dad.

Words to help me:
sorry
tell
talk
friends
explain
think
share
feelings

....

....

....

....

....

Turn over and draw a picture of yourself helping your friend to tell their family how they are feeling.

How do you feel when you have listened and tried to help?

I read and checked my work carefully.

Signed...date........................

Being Confident

This section contains: parents' notes,
a cover sheet for children to decorate
and the following activities.

- ▸ I can do this well
- ▸ Sam and Emil
- ▸ Good games
- ▸ A new skill
- ▸ A good rule for Isa
- ▸ Well done everyone

Being Confident

Parents Notes

These activities aim to help children to become more confident in who they are and what they can do. By emphasising children's strengths and reminding them how well they can do the things they do well, we make sure that the children feel good about their achievements. This 'feel good' factor will help them to take on board more challenging work with confidence.

This section contains the following activities:

- I can do this well
- Sam and Emil
- Good games
- A new skill
- A good rule for Isa
- Well done everyone

First, encourage your child to decorate and colour the enclosed cover sheet. We suggest that as you receive each activity sheet you find time to sit down in a quiet place with your child and read through it together. Help your child to understand and remember the words in the word list and use this list to write in spellings of other words your child chooses to use. You will find that some sections suggest ways to enhance the work on the sheet with ideas for you to talk about with your child.

▸ **I can do this well**

Helping your child to remember what s/he can do well is a great boost to confidence. You can help your child considerably if you make much of little successes and play down any 'failures'.

▸ **Sam and Emil**

It is often easier for children to solve problems if they are presented as a story. Here we meet Sam and Emil, and think about how they tackle a new skill. Talk about how they approach this new learning. Which do you think will be the most successful? Talk about a new skill that your child has recently had to learn. Remind her/him that learning any new skill needs lots of experience and practice before you are confident.

▸ **Good games**

Talk first about games you play with your child and as a family – card games, draughts, dominoes and bought games. These all have rules to learn and give confidence once learned. You can include construction kits and making things, computer games, playing trains etc. You may need to help with thinking of a new game using a ball.

▸ A new skill

There are stages in learning a new skill. After finding out about it and learning from people, then experiencing it, the final stage is practice and more practice. Determination plays a large part, and perseverance. It is often all too easy to give up. Talk about your experience of learning a skill – learning to drive or play football or tennis.

▸ A good rule for Isa

Meet Isa (boy or girl) who needs help at school. Talk about the six pieces of advice – all are essential – so any answer is correct! Here you are indirectly helping your child to focus on the skills s/he needs. The 'turn over' activity will help your child to feel good by helping Isa.

▸ Well done everyone

This sheet is another confidence booster – a reminder of the value of praise. Talk about what happens in your child's school when people have done something really good, and how achievements are recognised. Talk, too, about what happens at home. Talk about a smile or a gesture as a form of praise, we don't always need something tangible, just an acknowledgement.

Being Confident

This is me showing I am confident.
I stand tall and look people in the eye.
I believe in myself.

I can do this well
Sam and Emil
Good games
A new skill
A good rule for Isa
Well done everyone

I can do this well

Draw yourself doing something you can do well.

Write what you are doing.

Words to help me:
reading
running
skipping
swimming
riding
teacher
mum
dad
drawing

This is me ....

Who helped you to learn to do this?

....

How do you feel now you can do it?

I feel ....

Turn over and draw yourself telling someone about what you are good at. What are you saying?

I read and checked my work carefully.

Signed...date........................

Sam and Emil

Sam likes to learn new things and tries hard. Emil thinks learning new things is too hard and doesn't try to learn. They are both going for their first swimming lesson today.

Draw Sam in the water.

Words to help me:
fun
splash
deep
warm
trying
hard
scared

Draw Emil in the water.

How do you think Sam is feeling in the water?

I think Sam is feeling.............................

How do you think Emil is feeling?

I think Emil is feeling.............................
....

What would you say to Emil? ....

Think about Sam and Emil. Who is going to learn to swim first? Why do you think that?

Turn over and draw yourself learning a new skill. Are you most like Sam or Emil?

I read and checked my work carefully.

Signed..date..........................

Good games

When I was four years old I could play these games:

1..

2..

3..

Who helped you to play? ....

....

How did you feel when you won?

....

Now I am..years old,

I like this game...

This game was easy/hard to learn.

This is how you play it...

....

Think of a new game for two people using a ball.
Write down how you play it.

First you have to ....

....

Words to help me:
great
happy
pleased
satisfied
throw
catch

Turn over and draw yourself playing a good game with your friends. Write down where you play. Write down how you learned to play the game.

How do you feel when you lose? How do you feel when you win?

I have read my work and checked it carefully.

Signed..date........................

A new skill

When I want to learn something new, this is what I do:

First I ....

Then I ....

It is sometimes hard to learn a new skill and at first you feel...

....

But when you have learned a new skill you feel...........

....

What would you say to someone having difficulty in learning something new?

I would say ....

....

Words to help me:
find out
read
try
practise
ask for help
again

Turn over and draw yourself doing something you have just learned to do. Write why you wanted to do this. Who helped you?

I have read my work and checked it carefully.

Signed..date.........................

A good rule for Isa

Isa has problems with some new work in school. The teacher tries to help but Isa doesn't always listen. Isa thinks it's too hard, so it's not worth trying.

Isa's friends want to help. This is what they say. Which do you think is the best advice?

Words to help me:
neat
dictionary
spell
careful
ask
try
waste
time
pen
pencil

- Listen to the teacher

- Think about what the teacher means

- Get started at once

- Be careful

- Think hard

- Concentrate

I think ....

is best because...

....

....

Draw Isa trying to work hard.

Can you think of a good rule for Isa?

A good rule for Isa is ....

....

How do you think Isa feels when the teacher says, "Well done, Isa."

I think Isa feels..

Turn over and draw yourself helping Isa. How do you feel when the teacher is pleased with the work?

I read and checked my work carefully.

Signed...date.........................

Well done everyone!

The children in Class 4 have been working hard learning about Victorians. They have done an assembly for the whole school and their parents. Their teacher is really pleased.

He says ....

....

The headteacher is really pleased.

She says ....

....

The children are really pleased. How can they celebrate?

I think they can..

The children are designing some badges for good work. Can you finish them?

Words to help me:
well done
worked hard
rejoice
splendid
successful
special
share
party
certificate
award

Turn over and draw your family celebrating because they are so pleased with you.

How does that make you feel? (You could also design your own badge.)

I read and checked my work carefully.

Signed..date........................

Relationships

This section contains: parents' notes, a cover sheet for children to decorate and the following activities.

- ▸ Why I like you
- ▸ People like me when…
- ▸ People I trust
- ▸ Zoz needs help
- ▸ Is this bullying?
- ▸ Under the surface

Relationships

Parents' Notes

These activities aim to help children understand the importance of forging good relationships with people they know and new people they meet. This is an important skill on which their happiness and success will depend in their later school life and after school. People they will meet and need to relate to in the future will come from all walks of life and from various cultures and religions. These activity sheets can serve as useful starting points for family discussion.

This section contains the following activities:

- Why I like you
- People like me when…
- People I trust
- Zoz needs help
- Is this bullying?
- Under the surface

First, encourage your child to decorate and colour the enclosed cover sheet. We suggest that as you receive each activity sheet, you find time to sit down in a quiet place with your child and read through it together. Help your child to understand and remember the words in the word list and use this list to write in spellings of other words your child chooses to use. You will find that some sections suggest ways to enhance the work on the sheet with ideas for you to talk about with your child.

▸ **Why I like you**

This is an easy activity sheet to start with. Talk about the people you like and why you like them. Talk about how it is easy to like some people and quite difficult to like others. Why is this? Is it possible to find something likeable about even those people?

▸ **People like me when...**

This activity sheet asks your child to think about how other people relate to her/him. Help your child to realise that it is what people **do** that can help relationships along. If you smile, people will smile back – and the opposite is true.

▸ **People I trust**

Talk with your child about all the important people who are part of your 'circle' – the people you know you can depend on. Your child's best friends will come into this category. S/he also needs to know the people to trust outside this circle – those in authority or who have a special role to play – doctor, dentist, play leader, sports leader. No doubt the person your child trusts most of all will be you.

- ▶ **Zoz needs help**
  People come in all shapes and sizes and from all kinds of backgrounds. We are not at all like Zoz! Talk first about the variations between people you know – some may have different physical characteristics, others may have different racial or cultural backgrounds. This sheet will give you and your child the opportunity of looking together at the wider issues of race, religion and culture.
- ▶ **Is this bullying?**
  The nature of bullying is often difficult for children to recognise. Talk about what the children in the activity sheet think bullying is and whether they are right. Talk about the words in the 'help me' list. Talk about what your child should do if they see anyone being bullied or are being bullied themselves.
- ▶ **Under the surface**
  After reading through the activity sheet talk about how we are all the same underneath, but that we are all different, unique and special. Your child will meet people with special needs – mental and physical as well as meeting people who have different racial, cultural and religion backgrounds. Your child needs to know how to act when meeting people who look different in some way – those with facial disfigurements or who need help or equipment to lead a normal life.

Relationships

This is a picture of someone
I like very much.

Their name is: ....

Why I like you
People like me
People I trust
Zoz needs help
Is this bullying?
Under the surface

Why I like you

Think about someone you like very much.
Draw them here.

Words to help me:
friend
kind
safe
helpful
share
play

I like this person because ....

....

....

....

....

Turn over and draw yourself doing something to please this person.

What are you doing? How does the person feel? How do you feel?

I read and checked my work carefully.

Signed...date........................

People like me when...

My family like me when ....

....

My class group like me when.................................

....

My teacher likes me when....................................

....

The mid-day supervisor likes me when.......................

....

The caretaker likes me when.................................

....

Words to help me:
help
think
share
careful
tidy
messy
co-operate

Turn over and draw yourself doing something to please one of these people.

How does the person feel? How do you feel?

I read and checked my work carefully.

Signed...date........................

People I trust

Think about people special to you, people you can trust to help you when you need support. Who are these people?

I trust ....because I know

they...

....

I trust ....because I know

Write in this box the names of other people you know you can trust. if you don't know their names you can write their job, e.g. police officer

....

....

....

....

....

Words to help me:
safe
kind
family
friend
tell
listen
help
guide
fair
honest
true

Turn over and draw a picture of the person you trust most of all.

Write their name and how you feel when you are with this person.

I read and checked my work carefully.

Signed...date.......................

Zoz needs help

A robot called Zoz has come to visit your class and you are trying to explain about humans. Humans may look different and come from different countries but inside they are all the same (even though each one is unique and special).

Zoz says: Robots all look the same. How are humans different?

You say: Humans look different..

....

Zoz says: Robots come from the same factory. Do humans all come from the same factory?

You say: Humans come from ....

....

Zoz says: Robots are all programmed to act the same. How are humans different?

You say: Humans are not programmed. We ....

....

Zoz says: Robots have no feelings. How are humans different?

You say: Humans have feelings. We ....

....

Words to help me:
body
shape
happy
beautiful
countries
skin
hair
think
ourselves
others
hurt
choice

Turn over and draw a picture of Zoz. What else would you tell Zoz about humans? How do you feel when Zoz understands what you mean?

I read and checked my work carefully.

Signed...date........................

Is this bullying?

Tara is teasing her kitten by making loud noises and making the kitten jump.

Is this bullying? yes ☐ no ☐

Fred is calling a new boy names because his school clothes are different.

Is this bullying? yes ☐ no ☐

Sara is shouting when they are playing a game and says she won't play unless she can have her own way.

Is this bullying? yes ☐ no ☐

No one will play with May because she is spiteful and horrid to people. She says people are bullying her.

Is this bullying? yes ☐ no ☐

Words to help me:
tease
unkind
unfair
hurt
behaviour
force
persuade

In this box write down what you think bullying is.

I think bullying is ....

....

Show your work to a grown-up to see if you agree.

Did you agree?

Turn over and draw and write about what you would do if you saw someone bullying someone. How would doing this make you feel?

I read and checked my work carefully.

Signed...date.........................

Under the surface

Everyone is different. Think of two people who have some special difference and why you like them.

....

....

The first one is done for you and will help you.

Jojo comes from a different country, but I know Jojo is just like me – friendly and kind.

Words to help me:
walk
talk
play
colour
hair
language
customs

1 ....is different because

....

but underneath ....

....

2 ....is different because

....

but underneath ....

....

Turn over and draw someone on TV who is different. What are they like underneath?

I read and checked my work carefully.

Signed...date.........................

Empathy and Sympathy

This section contains: parents' notes, a cover sheet for children to decorate and the following activities.

- ▸ Someone new
- ▸ Missing him
- ▸ We can help
- ▸ How do they feel?
- ▸ Poor Jo
- ▸ In someone else's place

Empathy and Sympathy

Parents' Notes

These activities aim to help children think of the feelings of other people – to put themselves in their place as it were. Sometimes children act thoughtlessly to others because they do not think of the impact of their own actions on other people. One of the skills they will require if they are to grow into confident and well adjusted citizens is the skill of empathising and sympathising with others. In this section we meet a lot of new children. Help your child to empathise with their problems or situations.

This section contains the following activities:

- Someone new
- Missing him
- We can help
- How do they feel?
- Poor Jo
- In someone else's place

First, encourage your child to decorate and colour the enclosed cover sheet. We suggest that as you receive each activity sheet, you find time to sit down in a quiet place with your child and read through it together. Help your child to understand and remember the words in the word list and use this list to write in spellings of other words your child chooses to use. You will find that some sections suggest ways to enhance the work on the sheet with ideas for you to talk about with your child.

▸ **Someone new**
Read through the sheet and talk about how a new child could feel in a strange place where s/he doesn't know anyone or the rules of behaviour. If they have ever had to move to a new school they may well know how the new child feels. Your child will feel good about helping the new child to settle – it will be good for your child's self-esteem.

▸ **Missing him**
Talk about 'special needs' – what they are, and how children sometimes have to go away to be specially taught so they can cope with the real world on their own terms. Talk then about how someone like Dora would feel when her brother went away for whole terms at a time. Can your child put her/himself in the place of Dora? Or of Dora's brother?

- **We can help**
  This activity sheet asks your child to think of another new child, Zelda, who is not only new, but is 'different' in some way. Talk about the kinds of ways that Zelda can be different. Talk about the difficulty of accepting a new and special child into their group at playtime and in school. Can your child put her/himself into Zelda's place and think about how Zelda feels?

- **How do they feel?**
  Talk about the three children who have these varied problems. Does your child know how they would each feel? Ask your child to close their eyes, put her/himself in their place and show you by their face how the children feel. Can your child tell you this? – you may have to help out with some new words.

- **Poor Jo**
  Talk about Jo's feelings when the kitten is lost and also when it is found. You could also ask how the kitten feels! This gives you an opportunity to talk about a time when you or your child lost something (or someone) very dear.

- **In someone else's place**
  First think about the feelings of everyone in Pip's family. Can your child put her/himself in Pip's place, in Mum's place, in the new Dad's place and in the new brother's place? This activity sheet gives you the opportunity to talk about how everyone feels when there is a change in the family circle

Empathy and Sympathy

This is me thinking about how my teacher is feeling when we are all very good at school.

Someone new
Missing him
We can help
How do they feel?
Poor Jo
In someone else's place

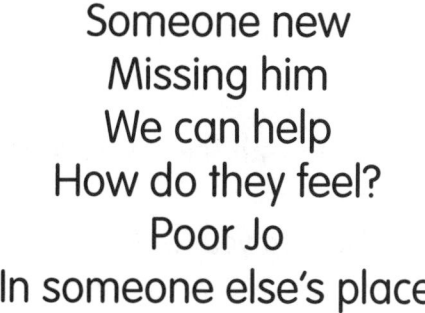

Someone new

A new child has just come into your class. They feel sad and lonely.

Words to help me:
kind
share
feel
help
work
play

How can you help this new child to feel better?

I can ....

....

Turn over and draw your friends playing with the new child in the playground.

How does the new child feel now? How do you feel?

I read and checked my work carefully.

Signed..date........................

Missing him

Dora's brother has special needs and has gone to a special boarding school so he won't be there for her at school or at home any more.

Draw a picture of Dora.

How do you think Dora is feeling?

....

I think Dora is feeling...

....

What can you say to Dora? ....

I'd say...

How can you help Dora to feel better?

I could ....

Turn over and help Dora to write a letter to her brother at his new school.

How does Dora feel now? How do you feel?

I read and checked my work carefully.

Signed...date........................

We can help

Zelda has just come to your school. She has been to lots of schools and finds the work hard. She looks different and feels different. She is sad and lonely. Can you help?

I can help Zelda in the classroom by ....

....

....

In the playground we can ....

....

....

In the dining room we can ....

....

....

In the after school club we could ....

....

....

Words to help me:
showing
sharing
kind
thinking
feelings
accept

Turn over and draw you playing with Zelda and other friends at your birthday party

How does Zelda feel? How do you feel?

I read and checked my work carefully.

Signed...date ....

How do they feel?

Jon's best work was spoiled when someone spilt paint all over it. How does Jon feel?

I think Jon feels ....

What can you say to Jon?

I'd say..

Borj has lost his dinner money on the way to school. How does Borj feel?

I think Borj feels ....

What can you say to Borj?

I'd say...

Zara's old dog is very ill and she thinks it will die. How does Zara feel?

I think she feels ....

What can you say to Zara?

I'd say...

....

Words to help me:
showing
sharing
kind
thinking
feelings
accept

Turn over and draw what Jon, Borj and Zara could do to make themselves feel better.

What do you do when sad things happen? Does that make you feel better?

I read and checked my work carefully.

Signed...date.......................

Poor Jo

Jo has had a kitten for three weeks and now it is lost. All the family have been helping to look for it. Jo thinks it might have been run over.

How do you think Jo is feeling?

I think Jo feels..

What can you do to help Jo?

I can ....

What do you think Jo will do when he gets home from school?

I think Jo will ....

Jo is making a poster. Can you help? Draw the kitten and write a description

Words to help me:
sorry
unhappy
worried
afraid
look
everywhere
better
happy
relieved

LOST - A kitten

It's name is ....

It's fur is ....

It's eyes are.........................

If you have seen it, please...........................

Turn over and draw someone bringing the kitten back

How do you think Jo feels now? How does the person who brought it back feel?

I read and checked my work carefully.

Signed..date.........................

In someone else's place

Pip is having a new Dad and two new brothers. Pip thinks that Mum might like the new brothers more and won't have time for her any more. Pip decides not to be friendly to the new people in the family.

Put yourself in these people's places and think how they would feel. How do you think Pip feels?

I think Pip feels ....

I think Mum feels ....

I think the new Dad feels ....

....

I think the new brothers feel ....

....

What could Pip do so that everyone gets on and feels happy in their new family?

Pip could try to ....

....

Words to help me:
worried
unhappy
unkind
awkward
unhelpful
think
feelings

Turn over and draw Pip and the new family being very happy together.

What are they doing? How do you think Pip feels now?

I read and checked my work carefully.

Signed..date........................

Co-operation

This section contains: parents' notes,
a cover sheet for children to decorate
and the following activities.

▸ This is my group
▸ We help each other
▸ I work with my family
▸ Keep to the rules
▸ Rules of friendship
▸ Celebrate success

Co-operation

Parents' Notes

These activities aim to help children to recognise the importance of co-operating with each other at school and outside school. Children need to learn this skill if they are to work with friends and family in harmony, now and in the future. Children who are co-operative will find learning easier and will feel good about themselves because of this.

This section contains the following activities:

- This is my group
- We help each other
- I work with my family
- Keep to the rules
- Rules of friendship
- Celebrate success

First, encourage your child to decorate and colour the enclosed cover sheet. We suggest that as you receive each activity sheet, you find time to sit down in a quiet place with your child and read through it together. Help your child to understand and remember the words in the word list and use this list to write in spellings of other words your child chooses to use. You will find that some sections suggest ways to enhance the work on the sheet with ideas for you to talk about with your child.

▸ **This is my group**
   Talk about the children your child plays with and works with at school. Your child will work in a small group at school and is asked to draw these children. Does your child find it easy to co-operate? Talk about how s/he feels after helping someone at school – how the people they help feel and how the teacher feels.

▸ **We help each other**
   Your child will work with different partners in some school activities. Talk about the importance of working together as a pair, helping each other and sharing ideas and equipment.

▸ **I work with my family**
   Talk about what your child does to help your family at home. Does s/he have some special responsibilities? Are these clearly defined? Does s/he 'earn' pocket money in some way. Talk as well about the general help that your child or children do in your house. Help your child to understand that they have a very real part to play in making their home a happy place.

- ▸ **Keep to the rules**

  Talk about rules around in school and at home, why there are rules, why we should obey them and what could happen if we didn't. An opportunity to talk about who makes the rules in and around your community.

- ▸ **Rules of friendship**

  More rules to discuss – this time the unwritten rules of friendship. Your child may need help in thinking about these – being loyal and truthful, sharing and caring, putting friends first, keeping promises, co-operating and many more. Your child is asked to share this work with everyone at home to see if they agree. It could provoke a family conference!

- ▸ **Celebrate success**

  This final activity sheet helps you and your child to talk about how you celebrate and how (and with whom) you share the good things that you achieve. Talk about successes of other family members and how you celebrated them. Remind your child that working hard and achieving success is a reward in itself. Celebrating this success promotes good self-esteem.

Co-operation

This is a picture of me co-operating with my family at home.

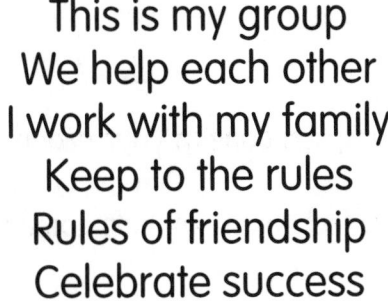

This is my group
We help each other
I work with my family
Keep to the rules
Rules of friendship
Celebrate success

This is my group

Draw a picture of the people in your working group.

Words to help me:
good
kind
helpful
share
ideas
spellings
words

These people are in my group.

Write their names in this box.

....

....

....

....

Turn over and draw yourself helping someone in your group

What are you doing? How do you feel when you help someone?

I read and checked my work carefully.

Signed...date........................

We help each other

Draw yourself working with a partner at school

Words to help me:
writing
doing
maths
game
activity
sharing
together
ask

Their name is ....

What work are you doing?

We are ....

How do you help each other?

We can ....

What do you do if you both can't do your work?

We ....

Turn over and draw yourself working with a partner in PE.

What are you doing? How do you feel when you work together?

I read and checked my work carefully.

Signed...date........................

I work with my family

Draw yourself doing something to help at home

Words to help me:
tidy
job
books
PE kit
folder
sensible
pleased

What are you doing?

I am...

....

How does this help your family?

It helps my family ....

....

Write down something that you are responsible for at home.

I am responsible for.......................................

How do you remember to do this?

....

Turn over and draw yourself getting things ready for school.

How do you feel when you remember to take everything you need?

I read and checked my work carefully.

Signed...date........................

Keep to the rules

Think of all the different places where you go and the rules there. Write down one rule for each of these places and then write two more rules that you think are important.

One rule in the library is ....

One rule at the swimming pool is ....

....

One rule at home is ....

One rule in the park is...

....

One rule near roads is ....

....

One rule on a bike is ....

....

One rule I think is important is ....

....

The other rule I think is important is.......................

....

Words to help me:
remember
quiet
running
help
grass
swings
listen
helmet
classroom
dinners
playground

Turn over and draw yourself keeping one of these rules.

Write what it is. How do you feel when you know the rules and keep them?

I read and checked my work carefully.

Signed...date.........................

Rules of friendship

Think of all the friends you have at home and at school.

Think of the unwritten rules that your friendship groups use so that they stay good friends. Write down three friendship rules and illustrate them. The first one is started for you.

Rule 1. Always stick by your friends.

Words to help me:
talk
listen
share
play
work
help
time
first
bossy
kind

Rule 2. . . . .

Rule 3. . . . .

Turn over and think of a rule for working together with your friends at school. Write this rule down. How you feel when you keep this rule and do really good work?

I read and checked my work carefully.

Signed. . . . . .date. . . . .

Celebrate success

You have gained a certificate for doing something really well.

Think about what this can be. ....

....

Write down what you think someone would award you a certificate for.

I think...

Who would you tell about this?

I would tell ....

Where would you put the certificate?

I would put it ....

Who would you celebrate with?

I would celebrate with ....

How would you celebrate this success?

I would...

Words to help me:
football
music
drama
swimming
dancing
behaviour
camping
holiday
talent
contest

Turn over and draw the certificate that you have won – put your name on it.

Write down what you did to earn this certificate – did you have to work very hard? How do you feel now you have got it?

I read and checked my work carefully.

Signed...date.........................

Letters and References

This section contains:
- ▶ Letters to parents
- ▶ Reminder letter
- ▶ List of picture story books
- ▶ Resources

Because I'm Special

A Take Home Programme to Enhance self-esteem

Dear

We know that it is important for children to have good self-esteem and to feel that what they do is valued. Some children are good at maths, some at writing, some at sports, art or craft. What we have to do is recognise and value the work and skills of each individual child. We know that children learn more easily and work better if they feel good about themselves and if they know that they are all special in some way.

Right from the children's first days in school, we are trying to help young children to understand the importance of valuing themselves and others. We try to help them to understand and deal with their own feelings and emotions. We give opportunities for them to co-operate with other children in work and play. We try to help children to respect other people's emotions and feelings.

We help them to learn, too, that everything they do can have a consequence for themselves as well as for other people. We help them to develop the skills they need to form relationships.

All these skills depend on good self-esteem and good self-esteem depends on them. If we can develop these skills in children, we go a long way towards giving them a firm foundation for their future adult lives as useful, caring, sensitive and fulfilled citizens.

Raising self-esteem among children will only work if all adults – teachers, parents, carers and others – take care about the self-esteem of other people. Children see much more than we realise and will quickly tune in to a feeling of a lack of respect among adults – or lack of care about each others' feelings.

We will be working with the children on developing their self-esteem through lessons and through some activity sheets that the children will bring home. We hope that you will help your children with the work on these activity sheets, talk around each theme and show your child that you value their work. These activity sheets are yours to keep. You may like your child to keep some of them in a folder or display them in their personal space in their own room.

Don't hesitate to contact me if you would like to discuss any points.

Best wishes

letter to parents – Because I'm Special

To the family of ....

We are doing some work about self-esteem in our class. When children have good self-esteem and feel that what they do is valued, they learn more easily and work better because they feel good about themselves.

In this work in school, we are trying to help young children to understand the importance of valuing themselves and others. We try to help them to understand and deal with their own feelings and emotions. We give opportunities for them to co-operate with other children in work and play. We try to help children to respect other people's emotions and feelings. We help them to learn, too, that everything they do can have a consequence for themselves as well as for other people. We help them to develop the skills they need to form relationships.

All these skills depend on good self-esteem and good self-esteem depends on them. If we can develop these skills in children, we go a long way towards giving them a firm foundation for their future adult lives as useful and fulfilled citizens.

We feel that it is very important to have your support in this and are asking for your help. We are using some 'take home' sheets for you to help your child with at home. The idea is for you and your child to work together to talk, not only about the work ,but also to talk about how the work relates to you, your child and your family. The finished work is for the children to keep at home – we do not want it to be returned.

There are six activity sheets in each section and before we send the first one home we will send a cover sheet and details about the six sheets to give you and your child help in doing the work. You can use the cover sheet and the sheets to make into a book, or you might prefer to encourage your child to display the current sheet somewhere at home – perhaps in her/his bedroom, replacing each sheet with the next.

▸ How to use the activity sheets

Illustrations are intended for the children to colour in. Some have a design, some a part design, others are blank on purpose so that children who are creative can make their own design – some children may prefer just to colour between the lines.

Each activity sheet has a list with words to help. Talk about what these mean – they are not only intended as a spelling aid and are deliberately not in order for your child to copy into blank spaces on the sheet. Neither are they meant to use all the words – it is hoped that the given words will trigger other more personal and descriptive words for them to use instead. There is space in the list for you to add spellings of other words that your child needs.

Below the main work on the sheet your child is asked to do some work on the other side of the paper. This piece of work is more personal and can be as short or as long as you and your child wish.

At the very end of the sheet is a reminder to your child to read and check the work and then to sign that s/he has done so. This is another aid to self-esteem – just as painters sign their work, it is hoped that your child will feel proud to add their name to their work.

Thank you for your help.

Reminder letter

Dear Parents

We are now starting work on section ....

of the self-esteem programme entitled.................................

Over the next few weeks we will be sending activity sheets
home to help you to share in this work. Please talk about the
work with your child and help her/him to understand and do
the work.

We are enclosing the folder cover sheet for this section so
that your child can decorate it as a start to this work. We
suggest you keep this and the six activity sheets in a plastic
folder or envelope until the work is completed. If you wish
you could then staple the pages together to make a book.

You don't have to keep the work in a folder. You may prefer
your child to display each sheet somewhere on her/his
territory as a reminder of success, and to replace each sheet
with the next as the work progresses.

We hope that you enjoy working with your child in this way.

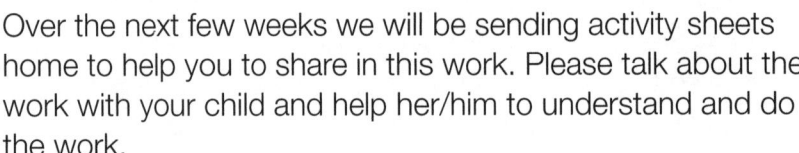

List of picture story books that support self-esteem

Amazing Grace, Mary Hoffman; Frances Lincoln. 1991
Badger's Bad Mood, Hiawyn Oram & Susan Varley; Picture Lions. 1999
Badger's Bring-Something Party, Hiawyn Oram & Susan Varley; Andersen. 1994
Daisy Rabbit's Tree House, Penny Dale; Walker. 1997
Dogger, Shirley Hughes; Red Fox. 1998
Don't forget to Write, M Selway; Red Fox. 1993
Dottie, Peta Coplans; Andersen. 1993
Elmer: the Story of a Patchwork Elephant, David McKee; Red Fox. 1990
Farmer Duck, Martin Wadell; Walker. 1995
I love you Blue Kangaroo, E.C.Clark; Andersen. 1998
It's Your Turn Roger, Susanna Gretz; Red Fox. 1996
Izzy and Skunk, Marie-Louise Fitzpatrick; David & Charles Children's Books. 2000
John Brown, Rose and the Midnight Cat, J Wagner; Picture Puffin. 1979
Jump, Magorian M; Walker Books. 1994
Katie Morag and the Tiresome Ted, Mairi Hedderwick; Red Fox. 1999
Little Beaver and the Echo, Amy MacDonald; Walker Books. 1993
Mary Mary, Sarah Hayes & Helen Craig; Walker. 1992
Mrs Gaddy and the Ghost, Wilson Gage; Bodley Head. 1981
Mrs Spoon's Family, Mallory Blacken; Andersen Press. 1995
My Great Grandpa, Martin Waddle; Walker. 2001
Nancy No-Size, Mary Hoffman and J Northway; Little Mammoth. 1990
Nothing, Mick Inkpen; Hodder. 1996
Omnibomulator, Dick King-Smith; Young Corgi. 1996
Orlando's Little While Friends, A Wood; Child's Play. 1981
Oscar got the blame, Tony Ross; Beaver. 1989
Oscar's Spots, Janet Robertson; Blackie. 1993
Piece of Cake, Jill Murphy; Walker. 1998
Pumpkin Soup, Helen Cooper; Picture Corgi. 1999
Ruby, Maggie Glen; Red Fox. 1992
Rumpelstiltskin, Helen Cresswell; Macdonald. 1998
Seal Surfer, Michael Foreman; Red Fox. 1998
Sheila Rae, The Brave, Kevin Henkes; Picture Puffins. 1990
Sing to the Stars, Mary B Barrett; Little, Brown & Co. Canada. 1994
Something Else, Kathryn Cave & Chris Riddell; Puffin. 1995
The Boy on the Beach, Niki Daly; Bloomsbury Publishing. 1999
The Huge Bag of Worries, V Ironside; Macdonald Young Books. 1996
The Nature of the Beast, Jan Carr; Tambourine Books. 1996
The New Boy, Keller H; Red Fox. 1994
The Patchwork Quilt, Valerie Flournoy; Puffin. 1995

The Travelling Musicians, P K Page; Viking. 1992

The Wild Washerwomen, John Yeoman; Hamish Hamilton Ltd, /Penguin. 1979

Timid Tim and the Cuggy Thief, John Prater; Red Fox. 1994

Two Monsters, David McKee; Beaver. 1987

What Else Can You Do?, Jean Marzollo Jerry Pinkney; Bodley Head. 1990

What Makes me Happy?, Catherine and Laurence Anholt; Walker. 1992

Why is the Sky Blue, Sally Grindley & S Varley; Hodder. 1998

Wilfred Gordon McDonald Partridge, Mem Fox; Penguin. 1987

Willy the Wimp, Anthony Browne; Little Mammoth. 1990

Windhover, Alan Brown & Christian Birmingham; Collins. 1998

Resources

Collins, M. (1995) *Keeping Safe* – safety education for young children. Forbes Publishing Ltd.

Collins, M. (1997) *Keep Yourself Safe* – an activity based resource for primary schools. Lucky Duck Publishing Ltd.

Collins, M. (1998) *Let's Get it Right for Nursery Children*. Forbes Publications.

Collins, M. (2001) *Because We're Worth It –*, Lucky Duck Publishing Ltd.

Collins, M. (2001) *Circle Time for the Very Young*. Lucky Duck Publishing, Bristol.

DfEE (2001) *Promoting Children's Mental Health within Early Years and School Settings*, Hunter, J. Phillips, S. and Wetton, N. (1998) *Hand in Hand* - Emotional Development through Literature, Progressive Printing, UK, Ltd

Milicic, Neva (1994) *It's good to be different* - Stories from the Circle Lucky Duck Publishing Ltd.

Qualifications and Curriculum Authority. (1999) *The National Curriculum Handbook* - for primary schools.

Robinson, G. & Maines, B (1995) *Celebrations* Lucky Duck Publishing Ltd

Wetton, N. & Collins, M. (1998) *Ourselves Resource Pack* (Watch). BBC Educational Publishing.

Wetton, N. & Collins, M. (1999) *Birth, Care and Growth Resource Pack* (Watch) BBC Educational Publishing

White, M. (1999) *Picture This – Guided Imagery* (CD, tape and booklet) Lucky Duck Publishing Ltd. Bristol

Visit www.wiredforhealth.gov.uk provides information for delivery of health education in schools

www.dfes.gov.uk/a-z/CITIZENSHIP.html

Margaret Collins is a teacher and former headteacher in infant/first schools. She is now Visiting Fellow at the Health Education Unit, Research and Development School of Education at the University of Southampton. She writes and co-writes teaching materials for children, books and articles on health education.

Don't forget to visit our website for all our latest publications, news and reviews.

www.luckyduck.co.uk

New publications every year on our specialist topics:

- **Emotional Literacy**
- **Self-esteem**
- **Bullying**
- **Positive Behaviour Management**
- **Circle Time**
- **Anger Management**
- **Asperger's Syndrome**
- **Eating Disorders**

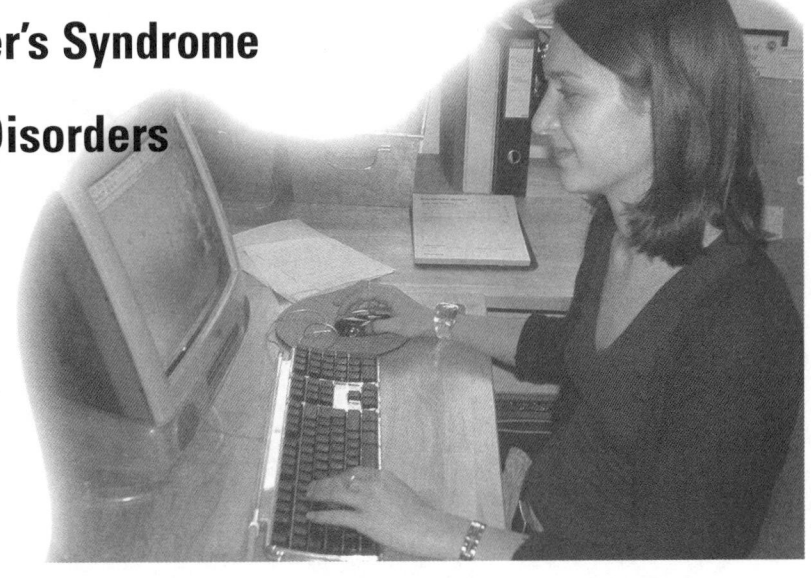